WEST MIDLANDS VOL I

Edited by Lucy Jenkins

First published in Great Britain in 1999 by
YOUNG WRITERS
Remus House,
Coltsfoot Drive,
Woodston,
Peterborough, PE2 9JX
Telephone (01733) 890066

All Rights Reserved

Copyright Contributors 1999

HB ISBN 0 75431 594 0
SB ISBN 0 75431 595 9

FOREWORD

Young Writers have produced poetry books in conjunction with schools for over eight years; providing a platform for talented young people to shine. This year, the Celebration 2000 collection of regional anthologies were developed with the millennium in mind.

With the nation taking stock of how far we have come, and reflecting on what we want to achieve in the future, our anthologies give a vivid insight into the thoughts and experiences of the younger generation.

We were once again impressed with the quality and attention to detail of every entry received and hope you will enjoy the poems we have decided to feature in *Celebration 2000 West Midlands Vol I* for many years to come.

CONTENTS

Guns Village Primary School

Adam Surplice	50
Faye Hewitt	51
Hayley Chisholm	51
Charlotte Preston	52

Joseph Turner Primary School

Lee Oakley	52
Mark Roper	53
Lucy Moore	53
Nathan Osborne	54
·Adam Scott	54
Gemma Jones	55
Johnathon Shelton	55
Richard Rudge	56
Gemma Perry	56
Lucy Howes	56
Amy Bastable	57
Ritchie Walton	57
Mitchell Davis	58
Jastinder Samra	58
Heather Summers	59
Shaun Barratt	59
Mitchell Green	60

Langley Primary School

Caroline Adams	60
Marie Adkins	61
Helen Skett	61
Anneka Davis	62
Manwinder Kaur Gosal	62
Amanda Thomson	63
Alisha Davis	63
Jodie Austin	64
Poonam Khosla	64
Ranveer Purewal	65
Luke Condley	66
Kelly Ann Averall	66
Gurpreet Sukhain	67

Keshia Bailey	68
Kerry Pugh	69
Kavita Prashar	70

Lapal Primary School

Chris Kelleher	70
Claire Dunn	71
Alex Penrose	72
David Kelleher	72
Timothy Seymour	73

Leighswood School

Jack Johnson	73
Jack Pemberton	74
Charlotte Bodin	74

Maney Hill Primary School

Katie Mulvey	74
Matthew Hathaway	75
Gagandeep Degun	76
Christopher Littler	76
James Barrell	77
Morgan Davison	78

Mount Pleasant Primary School

Aaron Griffin	78
Jemma Worsfold	79
Sophia Mifsud	79
Grace Zentilin	80
Luke Dawes	80
Steve Dunn	80
Danielle Smith	81
Jade Ross	81
Daniel Meredith	81
Jennifer Simmonds	82
Daniel Homer	82
Gabriella Zentilin	83
Matthew Simonian	83

Jamie Checketts	83
Kelly Parton	84
Paul Godwin	84
Lewis Mason	84
Holly Taylor	85
Stefan Davies	85
Daniel Orford	85
Olivia Hammond	86
Lloyd A Rose	86
Thomas Mullard	87
Christopher Griffin	87
Emma Jane Layland	88
Natalie McDonald	88
Michael J North	89
Charlotte Elise Harris	89
David Clarke	90
Iain Geddes	90
Harry Williams	91
Richard Bloomer	91

Peters Hill Primary School

Lucy Foster	92
Richa Okhandiar	92
Michelle Cartwright	93
Adèle James	94
Rebecca Glazzard	94
Jessica Calladine	95
Emma Leddington	95
Danielle Pearson	96
Thomas Hampton	97
Jonathan Siebert	98
Beth Lucas	98
Lauren Jasper	99
Christopher Del-Vecchio	100
Megan Dobson	100
Andrew Stevens	101
Katherine Tromans	101
Gregory Allen	102

The Poems

FROSTY DAYS

When the winter winds blow,
They go high and low,
They go here, there and everywhere.
Up, down, round and round,
Like a pound, spinning round.
Glitter here, glitter there,
It becomes everywhere,
It makes me very dizzy.
Red berries from holly,
Everyone's jolly.

Dawn Brown (9)
Birchills CE Primary School

COLD AND ICY DAY

Ice, ice, everywhere,
Where the chilly frost has been!
Spiders' webs glow, glow, glow,
And glitter all night.
When I look outside I see,
Frosty air coming near me.
When I go to bed,
I have to wear my muffs yet again.
When I think the frost has gone,
I see the snow, I think *oh no!*

Sonum Razaq (8)
Birchills CE Primary School

FROSTY DAYS

On frosty days when the ice glitters,
I always wear my fluffy blue mittens,
I see spider webs that shine,
I feel the coldness on the back of my spine,
I wear my thick coat that is red,
I feel like I want to go back to bed!

On frosty nights when the wind blows,
I always get a blocked-up nose,
On nights when I go to my nan's and it is chilly,
I get my teddy bear that I call Milly.

On frosty evenings when I have my tea,
I start to get cold and chilly,
When I go to play with my friends,
I wear my dark blue earmuffs yet again.

On frosty mornings when I get out of bed,
I feel the coldness in my head,
When I go downstairs to have my toast,
I feel cold, but chilly the most!

Samantha Chaunkria (8)
Birchills CE Primary School

INFANT SCHOOL DISASTER

Peter pushed past Pauline
And Pauline pushed Paul
So Peter pushed sideways
Then Pauline pushed them all.

Peter knocked the fire bell
And Pauline gave a shout
The dinner ladies heard them
And they all came running out.

They overturned their custard
And they tripped on their sprouts
And upset all their puddings
And upset their stew.

The shepherds pie went flying
The pig bins went as well
Then Pauline pushed past Peter
And tried to stop the bell.

Alex Brown (9)
Blue Coat CE Junior School

THE MAN FROM PERU

The man from Peru will come to you!
With wallpaper, carpets and windows too!
He's the handyman from Peru,
The man from Peru.

He climbs onto his private jet!
Listening to songs from Wet Wet Wet,
Somebody's in a fashion drama,
The patterns seem to melt him like lava.

He runs to the house that is soon
Going to get treated by the man from Peru.
He runs about fixing true,
It's hard work for the man from Peru!

So after a tiring day,
And he's tried his best in every way,
He's going to come to you,
He's the man from Peru!

James Loyns (8)
Blue Coat CE Junior School

THE WIND

Wind howling down chimneys and up the plughole,
Catapulting birds off their perches,
Howling, groaning, moaning wind.
Whirling leaves round into little whirlpools,
Blowing litter everywhere.
Slamming doors, banging, clanging,
Spraying water up high in the air,
Wild screams of children's voices.
On windy days that are rainy too,
The wind blows your umbrella inside-out,
Hats being blown off heads,
Leaves being torn from trees,
Flags and banners being ripped to pieces,
Fences and trees being blown over.
All is quiet, all is still,
The wind has passed over,
It's the end of the storm.

Rebecca Smith (8)
Blue Coat CE Junior School

DISNEY WORLD!

Oh Disney World! Oh Disney World!
Can I go to Disney World?
Will my dream ever come true?
To see Mickey visit his house,
To have tea and cake
Or maybe a milkshake.
To go in a hot air balloon
And shout to Mickey, 'See you soon.'
Then say to Mom and Dad,
'What a lovely time we had.'

Elizabeth Venner (8)
Blue Coat CE Junior School

4

UNDISCOVERED PLANET - SQUINCH

I can taste . . .
a strong mango and fished tuna from the seeds of
the tree that looked like a person with branch hands.

I can smell . . .
a strong disgusting watery oil that came from the
flask I had filled with Coke before I explored the
outer edge.

I can see . . .
pink leaves and oak trees and it was very much
like a jungle.

I can hear . . .
crunched branches and twigs being snapped as
I could hear someone coming towards me.

I can touch . . .
the big yellow pine trees and the
big green palm trees way over my size,
planet Squinch is absolutely gigantic and
absolutely brilliant.

I can feel . . .
a cold chill down my spine. I felt
unsure and like a wet soggy orange because we
had just discovered this 'undiscovered' planet
. . . Squinch!

Natalie Devey (9)
Blue Coat CE Junior School

THE MAN CALLED STAN!

Sitting in the sun, there was a man called Stan,
And after using butter had rather a blotchy tan,
It was red and mostly on his head,
And it hurt so much that he went to bed.

His wife tried it too and sat in the sun,
But missed a small patch on the side of her bum,
The patch was red and ever so hot,
It went all blotchy and turned to a spot.

Stan and his wife were a bit of a sight,
They couldn't go out and bathe in the light,
Him with his hetad and her with her bum,
They stayed in the house and looked at the sun.

Him with his head and her with her bum!

Chris Hitchcott (9)
Blue Coat CE Junior School

WHAT IS . . .?

What is red? Roses are red in a flowerbed.
What is green? Grass is green as it gleams.
What is blue? Sky is blue, I've got the flu.
What is yellow? Sun is yellow, I hate marshmallows!
What is orange? Oranges are orange, they're just orange.
What is purple? Berries are purple as they crumble.
What is pink? Skin is pink, but not ink.
What is black? Shoes are black as they clack.
What is white? Paper is white, what a sight!

William Haywood (8)
Blue Coat CE Junior School

THE COLOUR YELLOW

Yellow is perfect,
Yellow is the colour of colours,
Yellow brings peace and joy to everyone,
You can have yellow paper,
Yellow is the shining sun in the sky,
It is so brilliant!
Yellow is used for the colour of light,
Yellow is for the cat's golden yellow eyes
That shine in the dark.
A dinosaur's shining eyes in the wilderness,
Or some daffodils dozing in the sun.

Joshua King (8)
Blue Coat CE Junior School

WHAT IS BROWN? WHAT IS RED?

Brown is a Viking ship,
Brown is a piece of wood,
Brown is a cat walking down the street,
Brown is the wooden floor.

What is red?
Red is a red, red rose,
Red is a car whooshing by,
Red is the sunset as it awakes,
Red is a pencil crayon.

Ryan Derry (8)
Blue Coat CE Junior School

THE PEACEFUL FOREST

I can see green trees and bushes,
by the clear stream with tall shaking rushes.
I can see rabbits scampering around,
all over the purple heather ground.
I can hear foxes lapping water from the stream,
stamping down the grass that is bright green.
I can hear deer pounding everywhere,
going past the fox's lair.
I can touch the dainty anemones,
and the hard rough bark of the big oak trees.
I can touch the smooth petals of the daffodil,
and the tall green grass of the steep sloping hill.
I can smell the crocus creeping over the grassy floor,
while the cobwebs over the caves are acting like a door.
I can smell the ivy growing up the trees,
with its lovely dark green leaves.
I can taste the blackberries off their thorny bush,
they make a delicious pie after they've had a little crush.
I can taste honey from the bumblebees' hive,
the way it is shaking, it looks as if it's alive!

Candice Stevenson (9)
Blue Coat CE Junior School

THE FOREST BY DAY AND BY NIGHT

I can see orange foxes snoozing in their den
I can hear a woodpecker knocking a hole
I can touch wild red strawberries squashing in my hand
I can smell the lovely aroma of wild flowers
I can taste juicy blackberries.

I can see the moon on the silver birch
I can hear the hooting of an owl
I can touch the leaves rustling around
I can smell honey that bees have made
I can taste the raindrops dripping from the trees.

Jonathan Woodburn (9)
Blue Coat CE Junior School

FOREST BY NIGHT

I can see the misty clouds floating through the sky
I can see the dark shadows of the old trees
I can see the squirrels jumping from branch to branch
I can see the rabbits crunching on the plants
I can see the dazzling light shining through the leaves.

I can touch the silky grass that is soaking wet
I can touch the wild plants that are fragile
I can touch the rough trees with no leaves on
I can touch the smooth fur of the rabbit
I can touch the hard rocks rubbing against my hands.

I can hear the noisy woodpecker biting against the trees
I can hear the crunching as I tread upon the leaves
I can hear the small crickets hissing hard
I can hear the crashing rain as it hits the branches
I can hear the soft spider's legs crawling up me!

Alistair Davis (8)
Blue Coat CE Junior School

SELFISHNESS

We see the sad eyes of the crying babes,
We see the skin and bones of the hungry people,
With extended stomachs they seem to fade
Into distant memories like a church steeple.

We feel the pain for a day or two,
When we are reminded by those who care,
But what is there that we can do?
What do we have that we can share?

Our brothers in foreign lands wait for an annual thought,
Should we always take a stand
To provide for them who have nowt?

We are on this earth to defend each other,
To bring comfort where it's needed,
So remember the unfortunate who get into bother,
Because their sorrows and cries were not heeded.

Danielle McIntosh-Boothe (9)
Blue Coat CE Junior School

FRIENDSHIP

Friendship is about caring and sharing,
Friends are always loving and kind,
Friends are never bullies, but helpful,
They are always there when you need them,
They will play with you,
They never betray you,
So friendship is not about falling out,
But friendship is about staying together,
Friendship, friendship, everyone needs a friend.

Sarah Huckfield (9)
Blue Coat CE Junior School

THE FOREST OF FRIGHT

I can see a little striped bee
Collecting honey for the queen.
I can hear the droopy leaves
Fluttering in the breeze.
I can touch a little bluebell
Growing by an old well.
I can smell a little daffodil
Growing there as well.
I can see trees with faces,
Watch your paces.
I can hear and see a little fat wasp
Flying by the moss.

David Webb (9)
Blue Coat CE Junior School

THE ALIENS COME TO EARTH

Aliens coming to Earth,
Seeing the new things
The Earth has to show,
Changing course all the way.

Landing down on the runway,
Wondering what to do,
Following the cars,
Wondering where to go.

Finding all the restaurants,
Eating all the food,
Looking for some more,
They're in a funny mood.

Benjamin Cope (9)
Brandhall Primary School

SPACE

E arth is a big, round planet,
A steroids like Pluto,
R ed is the colour of Mars,
T elescopes to look into Space,
H ologram pictures made by dark craters and laser beams.

A erial for controlling lunar module,
N eptune the furthest planet from the sun,
D ynamo machine for producing electricity.

S olar panel, a large area for sun heating,
P ropulsion, the force for going forwards,
A ir on our Earth,
C onstellation is a group of stars,
E arth to live on.

B lue land Pluto,
E normous space where everyone goes,
Y ellowish moon,
O rangey Mars,
N eptune the planet,
D own on Earth for life.

Sophie Williams (8)
Brandhall Primary School

EARTH AND BEYOND

Space is the place where astronauts go,
To find out things that we don't know,
They have planets such as Jupiter and Mars,
And we can't get there in our cars.
Space has comets,
They are light,
And you will see them at night
And that is right.

Jessica Swoffer (8)
Brandhall Primary School

THE YOKE JOKE

At the centre of an egg is the yoke,
It might be serious, it could be a joke,
I'll sit down and think while I have a Coke.

It could be a yoke some people say,
It could be a chicken in a way,
If it's a crocodile, I'll run straight away.

The egg I brought cracked in the month of May,
It turned out to be a quaking day,
It took me ages to find out what it was,
But the day it cracked I knew. Do you?

David Barton (9)
Crestwood Park Primary School

FOOTBALL

Owen is the fastest runner
Better than Ole Gunnar Solskjaer,
Alan Shearer, England captain,
Dougie Freedman scores lots of goals,
Ginola, skilful, lives in Cornwall,
Beckham has really good kicks,
Muzzy Izzet, born in London,
Jimmy Floyd Hasselbaink likes scoring goals,
Gianfranco Zola in the Hall of Fame,
Kevin Davies, league star in the making,
Dwight Yorke, their top goal scorer.

Daniel Webb (9)
Crestwood Park Primary School

MY MUM

My mum makes me laugh,
When she's walking up the path.
My mum changes Ryan's nappy,
When the smell has gone, I'm really happy.

My mum does the washing up,
I never wash a cup.
My mum makes me smile,
And only nags me once in a while.

Richard Wheelwright (10)
Crestwood Park Primary School

MY MAGIC BOX

I will put in my box
the sound of a kitten miaowing,
the footprints in the mud of a dog,
a little baby bird that has just learnt to fly.

I will put in my box
the first purple pickle pepper,
the smell of nature outside,
the first two colours of the rainbow.

I will put in my box
the sound of Santa coming at Easter,
the sight of the Easter bunny coming at Christmas,
the touch of a cowboy wearing a silk dress.

My box is created from gold, silver and diamonds,
its hinges are the claws of a ginger cat.

I shall ride away in my box
on a white, galloping horse,
up and down the mountains,
then wash ashore on the back of a sparkling dolphin.

Sarah Firkin (9)
Dingle Primary School

HAIKU

Come on, it's raining
I am soaked right to my skin,
Where has the sun gone?

Emily Davies (8)
Dingle Primary School

HAIKU

It's a sunny day,
It was raining yesterday,
The sun has gone in.

Rachelle Sawyer (7)
Dingle Primary School

HAIKU

Snowman in a field,
Listening to the snowdrops,
Wishing them farewell.

Joshua Davies (7)
Dingle Primary School

HAIKU

Looking for a man,
Who is robbing a big shop,
He's taken the cans.

Thomas Cartwright (7)
Dingle Primary School

TEACHERS

T eachers are always giving you work as fast as a cheetah running
fifty miles an hour,
E very teacher I have had has normally always been kind like
a friendly person,
A ny hour before playtime they would keep us in like angry
crocodiles,
'C ome on!' they would say in a naughty ape way, they would
tell us 'Hurry up!'
H er hair is as bright as the moon that is shining in the dark sky,
E ven when it's dark she will light up like a bright star from
fifty miles away,
R eally my teachers are very nice, just like me and little mice.

Lauren Smart (8)
Dingle Primary School

COWBOYS INVADE

C owboys race like stripy zebras through small villages,
O nly mad cowboys invade villages like big, clumsy elephants,
W icked, powerful guns shoot straight like fast and rapid cheetahs,
B ut only mad people shoot innocent people like nasty criminals,
O n every day they fight for survival and guns like fierce lions
hunt for food,
Y ou're never in danger of dangerous Mexicans, like small and big
zebras are in danger of massive crocodiles,
S o evil Americans never give up and fight fiercely against other
deadly cowboys.

Joseph Allan (9)
Dingle Primary School

MY MAGIC BOX

I will put in my box -
A white sandy beach by the Atlantic Ocean
A dog barking for food
A sweet singing bird.

I will put in my box -
The sound of children playing in the playground
Christmas every day
A mouse chasing a cat.

I will put in my box -
The taste of fresh air
The sound of a cat purring
A smell of charming roses.

My box is fashioned from gold,
Silver and emeralds
with the waves of the Indian Ocean
On the lid and wishes in the corners.
Its hinges are the claws of a tiger.

I will fly in my box, in a hot air balloon
In the fresh air and land in a very warm bed.

Hannah Marsh (9)
Dingle Primary School

CLOWN

C lowns are happy
L ike a rainbow in the sky
O h they are as funny as the head mistress
W e go to the circus
N aughty as the teacher.

Stephanie Platt (9)
Dingle Primary School

Cowboys Attack!

C owboys destroy their little villages like clumsy elephants
   racing madly.
O nly cowboys have wicked guns like charging tigers.
W icked, hungry horses eat all day like fat pigs.
B ut only crazy cowboys have the best aim to shoot,
   the bullets come out like fast cheetahs.
O n every evening when the bright sun goes down,
   out they come and attack like fierce lions eating their prey.
Y ou're always in danger when the stupid cowboys come with
   their silly guns with bullets like cheetahs.
S o be warned whenever they come, surrender, don't fight,
   or they'll kill you as quick as a puma.

Nathan Westwood (9)
Dingle Primary School

The Poem Of My Sister

S ister, as stupid as a spaghetti-swinging monkey,
I n the brown house my sister drives me up the wall like a wild bear,
S miles like a clown in a colourful circus
T all as a bear, fat as a brick,
E ats like a wild bear in the forest
R ed as a strawberry when she gets hot.

Stacey Jones (8)
Dingle Primary School

BAD BROTHER

B ad as a hunting cheetah, as angry as can be,
R unning round the garden like a scared little mouse like me,
O n the Packard Bell computer working hard like a sweating
   forehead I see,
T apping on the sideboard treating me bad like an angry mom
   shouting at me,
H is ears are very hairy like a long-haired ape you see,
E ating like a greedy pig, smelly as can be,
R est in peace like a sleepy lion, zzzzzzzz.

Jessica Oakes (8)
Dingle Primary School

LIFESAVER

L ifesaver looks out for danger
I 'll race through the water like a bullet being shot out of a gun
F ebruary is a busy month for the staff
E ach year we are packed with people
S ounds of people were loud
A lmost time for the staff to go
V iew of the lifeguards
E very part has a member of staff there
R emember about the trouble.

Vanessa Morgan (9)
Dingle Primary School

CLOWNS' ACT!

C lowns have funny faces like a colourful rainbow shining in the sky
L oud as a grey elephant with a small mouse after him
O range balls juggling around like bunches of oranges falling
    off a very old tree
W hite snow was like their white faces, falling
N o one didn't like them, no one doesn't like big, grey elephants.

Richard Garbett (9)
Dingle Primary School

BROTHER

B rilliant at maths, like a brainwave,
R acing like a cheetah, running with all its speed,
O ften playing on the PlayStation like a chatty robot,
T hin as a peanut like an eaten pebble,
H as talent like a black superhero
E ats loud like a fat pig,
R ed as blood like a dead rat.

Nicholas Harbidge (8)
Dingle Primary School

CLOWN

C lown like a clumsy baby learning to walk
L ikes to dress up like some young little girls
O ld and silly like a little monkey
W ater they throw like a big wrinkly
N ever quiet like a noisy parrot that's learning to talk.

Luke Garbett (8)
Dingle Primary School

MY SISTER

S he is as dumb as a broomstick, very, very silly
I think she's a prune and black and brown
S tupid as a carrotstick that's orange and very, very sickly
T hose shoes are black and high and make her touch the blue sky
E ars are disgusting but very shiny earrings, but quite disgusted
R eads and writes alright, but not brilliant.

Becci Cox (8)
Dingle Primary School

WINTER

Snow will never melt
on cold and winter days
children play all day.

Stuart Poyner (9)
Dingle Primary School

HAIKU

Sue is fine today
Are you coming out to play?
Yes I can come out.

Kirstie Baker (8)
Dingle Primary School

MY MAGIC BOX

I will put in my box . . .
some slimy small serious snakes
and an elephant riding on a broomstick
you can hear the water
whooping and whirling

I will put in my box . . .
a big, roaring, rattling robot
a sound of a bird whistling in his tree
you can see a big, brown bear bellowing

I will put in my box . . .
a dragon letting out fire
the wind knocking a house down
a roaring horn beeping in a line.

I will put in my box . . .
a fish playing in a puddle
you can see a dog playing with a cat
and a cat blowing bubbles

I will put in my box . . .
some stars twinkling away
a sparkling tiger looking up at the sun
and a red dog talking

My box is fashioned with rubies
a slice from the sun and silver
in the corner, pieces of gold and diamonds
and moons on the lid
the claws of the dog holding it together

My box travels on a cloud
swooping in the sky and travels to a
splendid white beach near Africa.

Samantha Curtis (9)
Dingle Primary School

MY MAGIC BOX

I will put in my box
A buzzing bee still buzzing badly,
A wild wind whipping rapidly,
A sipping, snipping, soaking spider.

I will put in my box
A rolling, polling polar bear,
A snapping, sneaking, sulking snake,
A laughing, roaring, panting dog.

I will put in my box
A puddle puffing and panting,
A snapping cat barking all the time,
A clapping dog miaowing.

I will put in my box
A sweet that sparkles in the night,
The smell of a nose that rises in spring,
The taste of fish out of the sea.

I will put in my box
The bright colour of a firework blasting into Space,
The splashes from the sea as it reaches me,
The last bright blue sea.

My box is fashioned from coloured glass and
brass edges and a metal rainbow,
its hinges are the toe joints of a chicken.

I shall fly in my box
on the wild yellow beach,
then onto the tallest tower in the world,
and all the colours of the rainbow.

Amy Bradley (9)
Dingle Primary School

MY MAGIC BOX

I will put in my box
a bird that I can hear chirping in the night,
a crashing of floods from a waterfall,
using a sharpener for a rubber and using
a rubber for a sharpener.

I will put in my box
the racing people running round the course,
I can taste a jelly wobbling on a plate
that is clean and fresh,
the clock's going chirp, chirp.

I will put in my box
a man that can change into a baby in a minute,
a cat barking and a dog miaowing,
a carpet that flies in the air.

I will put in my box
the smell of roses in the morning,
a cowboy flying in the air,
a gorilla that speaks English.

My box is gold and grey with red stars on the lid,
and you can hear a whisper in the corner,
the hinges are made out of squirrels' feet,
I will return on a golden beach in Heaven.

Clare Haycock (9)
Dingle Primary School

HAIKU

To be a good friend
You have to be kind, helpful.
Gentle and so kind.

Jamie Lad (8)
Dingle Primary School

HAIKU

To be nice to you
And other people as well
And to be gentle.

Jenny Johnson (8)
Dingle Primary School

HAIKU

Aliens are green
Aliens love space and stars
They have a spaceship.

Todd Westwood (8)
Dingle Primary School

FUNNY CLOWNS

C lowns are stupid with red noses like a rainbow
L ong ago clowns laughed all the time
O range hair with a white face
W e go to the circus and see clowns
N aughty Nicky was the best of all.

Danielle Thompson-Webb
Dingle Primary School

HAIKU

My bedroom is clean
It can be messy sometimes
And it is spotless.

Carl Butcher (7)
Dingle Primary School

HAIKU

It has been snowing
I'm building a snowman
I gave him my hat.

Roxanne Ward (7)
Dingle Primary School

MY SISTER

S isters are grumpy in the morning, like a hungry lion
I n the house she drives me up the wall, like a mad monkey
S he plays marbles like a cheating cheetah
T idies her room and keeps it clean like a houseproud badger
E very day she eats like a starving baby elephant
R emember she is special to me - like a diamond ring.

Ross James Cooper (9)
Dingle Primary School

CLOWN

C lowns are funny, squirting water at you
L ittle clowns are funny too, with dummies in their mouths
O n the poles there are three acrobats
W ith the stools one elephant stands
N ext the horses circle the ring.

Martin Gwilliams (8)
Dingle Primary School

STUPID SISTER!

S tupid as thick yellow custard
I nk all over the place
S ticky white glue everywhere
T hrows red tomatoes wherever she goes
E ating like a pig as far as can be
R unning rings around crooked old Grandma.

Shaun Cadwalleder (8)
Dingle Primary School

I LOVE MY MOTHER

M y mother is like a loving bear
O h she is the most special person in the world
T he roses go by, but she's always there
H appy things never go away with my mother
E aster comes, Mother wakes up with a bright smile like hot sunshine
R oses are like Mother's skin, pink and soft.

Ceri Davies (9)
Dingle Primary School

FOOTBALL

Kick it in the net!
It's a goal! One nil to us.
The match is finished.

Gary Cartwright (9)
Dingle Primary School

SPRING

S pring makes me happy
P lants are growing
R abbits have babies
I nsects are hiding
N ice flowers are growing
G rass is strong and I am happy.

Melissa Swift (7)
Guns Village Primary School

EASTER

E aster's here - it's so exciting!
A t Easter everyone's crying
S tacks of Easter eggs
T errific tastes of the Easter eggs
E veryone's having fun
R ich golden wrappers.

I t's great fun eating chocolate
N ow have a box of it.

S tuff yourself 'cause it's Easter
P acks of Galaxy
R ich golden tastes
I t's yummy Galaxy
N o one could miss it
G oodness! Not a bit
T ime to eat
I t's a feast
M oms are great
E aster's the greatest time of all.

John Richards (8)
Guns Village Primary School

SPRING

Spring makes the sun come out
Spring is nice
Spring is beautiful
Spring is coming out today
Spring is nice because it's yellow
Spring makes the flowers grow.

Sunny Dutt (7)
Guns Village Primary School

EASTER TIME

E aster eggs are appearing for you
A round the Easter bunny that hops around at Easter time
S weets and fun, springtime is joyful
T eachers are happy because they have chocolate
E aster's here and children are happy too, they've got chocolates
   for you
R abbits are the ones we should thank for fun at Easter time.

T ime is the life at Easter time, a bunny rabbit at Easter
I like Easter eggs, thanks to the bunny rabbit
M any farmers are rushing around because chickens and sheep
                      are having babies at Easter
E aster is the best time of my life, because spring makes me happy.

Emma Cross (8)
Guns Village Primary School

EASTER TIME

E aster is lovely and cool
A nd a nice lovely time
S pring is a beautiful time of the year
T ime goes quicker at Easter time
E aster eggs are brown and white
R abbits come out of their burrows

T rees grow quickly
I t's a good time at Easter
M onkeys start to talk
E ggs are sweet and brown.

Luke Simms (8)
Guns Village Primary School

SISTERS

Sisters are sisters, but what are they for?
Are they for fighting - maybe more.
Here are the sisters Jill and Lill,
When they were three they fought over a tree.
You see this tree started growing when Jill and Lill were born.
Lill fed it rice and Jill fed it mice.
One day Lill and Jill moved to a country far away,
they did not want to leave the tree.
Mum said 'You can take the tree, but make sure you dress it properly.'
So Jill and Lill took it on the plane
the tree acted as if it was very vain.
Suddenly the plane nearly crashed, it swooped up high
people were saying *my oh my!*
The helper said *throw the tree off the plane!*
Jill and Lill were mad with anger
so they jumped off the plane with the tree
and landed in Maranda.
There in Maranda, they married a gander
and they lived happily ever after.

Anupa Patel (9)
Guns Village Primary School

SPRING

Spring is when flowers grow nice and shiny for you and me
Spring is when everything grows
Spring means that the leaves grow and the sun comes out
Spring is when you go out and play games
Spring is colourful and bright
Spring means there is new life.

Jasmin Arafa Khatun (8)
Guns Village Primary School

THE COOL DUDE

Do you wanna know a story of Ace?
He's cool because he comes from space.
He has peace from a lad called Lace.

      It's a cool dude's life
      It's a cool dude's life!

I am the best from the west
I like to eat a big feast
because I'm the beast from the east.

I am happy
I am smellier than a nappy.
I've got no education
not even the situation
but I've got an explanation
and I've got the indication.
I am the beast from the east.

      It's a cool dude's life
      It's a cool dude's life!

      His friend is the Rock
      He gives you a big shock.

Arundeep Malhi (9)
Guns Village Primary School

JAMES LAWRENCE

J am maniac
A rt attack
M ad maniac
E normously fat
S melly James

L aughing James
A rt mad
W onderful James
R eally mad
E normously dummy
N ever funny
C hocolate taste
E normously short

This is James!

Nathan Jones (9)
Guns Village Primary School

SPRING

S pring is fun
P eople are dancing
R ain is coming
I n the garden, birds are singing
N uts are growing on trees
G rass is shiny and I am happy.

Priyanka Patel (7)
Guns Village Primary School

SPRING

Spring means new you,
Spring is the flowers,
Spring is good,
Spring is nice,
Spring is like you,
Spring is colourful,
Spring is beautiful,
Spring is when eggs crack,
Spring - I love,
Spring is when flowers come out,
Spring is wonderful,
Spring is Easter,
Spring is when flowers grow big,
Spring is when the Easter bunny comes,
Spring is here.

James Williams (8)
Guns Village Primary School

DANCE CLASS

Get ready
    call a taxi
        change shoes
            Dance! Dance!
                heart racing
                    feet pacing
                        taxi home
                            feet aching.

Karina Patel (8)
Guns Village Primary School

SPRING

Spring is cold
Spring is beautiful
Spring is good
Spring is nice
Spring is colourful
Spring is life
Spring is lovely
Spring is excellent
Spring is rain
Spring is night
Spring is hot
Spring is happy
Spring is sunny.

Munpreet Bassan (8)
Guns Village Primary School

THE SIMPSONS

T he Simpsons are the best
H omer and the rest
E very day it is on.

S impsons live in Springfield
I love the Simpsons
M arge has her own car
P ete is Homer's best friend
S trict teachers they have in school
O nly on Sky One
N aughty Bart and Lisa
S ix till seven o'clock

Sandeep Patel (9)
Guns Village Primary School

MY MILLENNIUM RAP

Millennium is coming
My heart starts thumpin'
The sky turns blue
Millennium is due
Computers might crash
We'll end up in a hash
I wanna know what's happening
So let's start rappin'

Millennium is comin'
Millennium is comin'

If you wanna be smart
You gotta take part
We're at a big party
We'll all be hearty.

Millennium is comin'
Millennium is comin'
So let's all shout *the millennium is coming.*

Laura Mackenzie (9)
Guns Village Primary School

OUR SCHOOL

Our school is the best
And the cooks will beat the rest.
The teachers are cool
As well as the school
The teachers are cool
You could not choose another school.

Tanya Lowe (9)
Guns Village Primary School

A SORRY POEM

I really want to say to you.
My heart says it too.

Sorry everybody for everything I've done
once and for all deep down inside
I really want to say
remember it does take time, forgive me please
you just have to wait.

Everyone thinks I should say sorry
very few say so though.
Everyone should get a sorry, but
remember it does take time.
Forgive me please . . .
You would want me to forgive you
if it was you who had done wrong.
One more chance, that's all I'm asking you.
No more ifs or buts . . .
Everyone forgive me please.

I'm sorry everyone!

Kelly Louise Jewkes (9)
Guns Village Primary School

IN THE SUMMER

The summer is calming
It's fun
I love it so much
I will run, run and run.

The sun is hot
The flowers in my pot
They look so beautiful
But not like the sun.

Karandip Kaur (9)
Guns Village Primary School

THE TEENY TINY GHOST

A teeny, tiny ghost
no bigger than a mouse,
at most,
Lived in a great big house.

It's hard to haunt
a great big house
When you're a teeny, tiny ghost
no bigger than a mouse
at most.

He did what he could do.

So every dark and stormy night
the kind that shakes the house with fright -
if you stood still and listened right,
you'd hear a
teeny
tiny
boo!

Buta Sandhu (9)
Guns Village Primary School

EASTER'S HERE

E aster eggs are so chocolaty
A nd delicious when they want to be
S o eat your Easter eggs at Easter time
T ime for new life all over the farm
E at your lovely green grass says the farmer to the sheep
R ight away they eat their grass.
,
S oon they have their lambkins.

H eather starts to grow all over the place
E very other flower starts to grow
R esurrection from Jesus Christ
E ven brings life.

Joshua Hobday (8)
Guns Village Primary School

PLAYING COOK

I'm a cook today Sir,
How would you like to dine?
I've got ginger nuts for joints Sir,
And orange juice for wine.

Chocolate creams for puddings
And almond cake for cheese;
It's very nice indeed, Sir,
Just taste it if you please.

Mohammed Shazahan Rahman (9)
Guns Village Primary School

EASTER

E aster eggs are delicious and chocolaty too
A nimals have their babies in the farmyard too
S heep have their lambs so soft and fluffy
T rees start having leaves so bright and green
E ggs are cracking open and little chicks come out
R abbits have their bunnies so small and cute
'
S heep have their wool cut off and knitted

H amsters wake again from hibernation
E aster's when Jesus rose from the dead
R abbits go to find food for their kids
E very day is new.

Daniel Beard (8)
Guns Village Primary School

SPRING

Spring is coming
Spring is colourful
Spring is new life
Spring is when flowers grow
Spring is happy
Spring is Easter time too
Spring means animals are born
Spring is coming at Easter!

Katie Timmins (7)
Guns Village Primary School

IN THE SEA

In the sea - it is fun
because we splash in the sun.
In the sea there are dangerous species
like sharks and jellyfish.
But there are nice things too
like fishes and dolphins.
Dolphins jump high into the air
then land beneath, while you stop and stare.
In the sea there are weeds to tangle you up.
There are seals who bark to call their pups.
That's why it's fun in the sun.

Laura Walker (8)
Guns Village Primary School

I'M SORRY DAD

I'm sorry for all the things I've done.
Moaning so selfishly.
Saying the things I've said.
Or shouting the things I've shouted,
All I really want to say is *sorry*
I really want you to forgive me.
You mean a lot to me.
Dad please, don't be angry
And Dad please, please forgive me.
Dad I really am sorry.

Sophie Louise Hall (9)
Guns Village Primary School

SPRINGTIME

S pring is a happy time full of joy
P eople love spring because it's for happiness
R abbits come out to play
I t's a time for Easter eggs, hip, hip, hooray
N ew life for fluffy bunnies
G reat Easter eggs are sold
T weeties start to sing
I start putting up decorations for Easter
M agpies start searching for food
E aster eggs are yummy for your tummy.

Martyn Holland (7)
Guns Village Primary School

SPRINGTIME

S pring is a happy time
P retty flowers come out
R ainbows come out to play
I t's spring, have a happy time of year
N ew beginnings in spring
G ardens are pretty in spring.
T ime for days to last longer
I t's Easter in spring
M ore sweets come at Easter
E aster chicks crack out of their eggs.

Adam Davey (8)
Guns Village Primary School

Easter Time Is . . .

S ometimes people play in the sun
P eople eat Easter eggs
R ain stops pouring
I feel sick when I have loads of Easter eggs
N obody hates spring, they love it
G ood it's springtime
T wo more eggs to eat
I n spring the birds start singing
M y friend has had about fifty eggs
E verybody loves Easter.

Sanjeev Dass (7)
Guns Village Primary School

Spring

S pring, spring is a happy time
P retty flowers come out
R abbits and bunnies come out to play
I t's Easter, Easter - happy Easter
N ew life in spring
G ardens and flowers are pretty in spring
T his time of the year the new babies are born
I t's Easter in spring
M ore wild life in spring
E aster is when you get Easter eggs.

James Lee Ballam (8)
Guns Village Primary School

SPRINGTIME

Spring is here
People are full of cheer
Rain is up
In spring it's Easter
New lambs are born
Jesus was nailed to the cross
The time of Easter is here
My favourite time is spring
Easter is my best time too.

Happy spring and Easter too.

Harsharanpreet Kaur Thind (7)
Guns Village Primary School

MILLENNIUM FUTURE

Year 2000 has gone by.
Oh time does fly.
Year 2000 was a party beyond your imagination,
there was no hesitation.

Millennium come again.
It's a shame we'll be dead then.
Come again,
rise again,
shower us with happiness.

Next millennium,
robots will fly
and we will die.

Nicola Devereux (9)
Hall Green Primary School

THE YEAR 2000

The millennium is a time of happiness.
People yell and party all night long.
When the clock strikes twelve
people will cheer.
They will be drinking whisky and beer.

When the year 2000 comes,
we will be changing our life.
The computers will have a problem
with the Millennium Bug.
So let's have a
party and a great big hug.

Hayley Champion (9)
Hall Green Primary School

BOOM, BOOM

I was sitting in the TV room
When an alien came out of the gloom.
It gave me such a fright
As it went out of sight.
Then my heart went,
Boom, boom!

Emma Louise Hobbs (9)
Hall Green Primary School

THE MILLENNIUM

Let's all celebrate the millennium here;
people are drinking wine and beer.
It's the biggest party ever,
lots of people are wearing leather.

Let's dance and sing,
when the clock goes ting.
Let's go to a party outside,
and dance and sing with pride.

They're building the Millennium Dome;
but at the end we all go home.

Hannah Guttridge (9)
Hall Green Primary School

THAT POOR LITTLE CAT

There was a cat that got chucked out on the street,
It was cute and furry and ever so sweet.
That cat could see an open door,
He went in and he wasn't alone anymore.
A lady took the cat into her house,
And then he got a job trying to catch a mouse.

Charlotte Bradley (8)
Hall Green Primary School

MR OWL

Mr Owl lives in Humble Town,
and you'll never see him frown.
His job is a teacher
and he has to wear a funny crown.

I've always wondered how he could speak,
or how he could write on the blackboard.
How can he be such fun and never make people bored.
But once again he has to go and fill up with food,
with his claws as sharp as a small sword.

Kayleigh Veal (9)
Hurst Green Primary School

MILLENNIUM

M illennium is approaching.
I t's going to be great.
L et's go out and party,
L et's celebrate.
E njoy the festivities,
N oisy fireworks galore.
N..ow it's rockets and bangers
I n parks and in gardens,
U p skywards they soar.
M illennium!

Andrew Bladon (9)
Hurst Green Primary School

MY MONSTER

My monster likes to play jokes
on different kinds of folks.
He's got two eyes, a nose that's clear,
he always seems to disappear!

My monster likes chocolate, that's very hard to see.
He sometimes picks on people but he always picks on me.
I love my little monster, he has to be the best
but I think he is the naughtiest little pest.

Scarlett Martin (9)
Hurst Green Primary School

FLOWERS

Flowers are bright though they can be dull
but most of them are colourful.
They're around my garden and up the wall
but the flowers keep coming there's more and more.

But the best thing about them is when they sparkle in day showers.
Flowers are always here to have a celebration and a good cheer.
They would like a fan in the day
but then at night they sway away.

Lauren Boast (9)
Hurst Green Primary School

SPECKLE THE ADVENTUROUS DOG

Speckle is an adventurous dog.
He's often stepping on a log.
He lives in the hill and dale,
Speckle loves the white sparkling hail.

Speckle is a black and white hound,
He loves to pound around.
He has blue shiny eyes,
Speckle loves eating meat pies.

Speckle, a good dog is he.
He dances with his friend the bee.
They buzz and jump throughout the day,
Then go and rest on the hay.

Nina Howell (9)
Hurst Green Primary School

MILLENNIUM

It's the millennium next year
And everything is very dear.
When the bell chimed 12 o'clock
At the door there was a big knock.
Everyone shouted Happy New Year
Even the people that couldn't hear.

Adam Surplice (9)
Hurst Green Primary School

HARRY THE HOLIDAY HAMSTER

Harry the Holiday Hamster, travels everywhere,
Spending all his money without a blooming care.
He goes to Italy, New Zealand and Spain,
The holiday agents think he's a pain.

Harry is a palish brown,
He always smiles he never frowns.
At the moment he's cruising on a ferry,
Eating biscuits and drinking sherry.

Faye Hewitt (9)
Hurst Green Primary School

MAX THE LAZY RACING HORSE

Max supposedly is a racing horse; he's called the Lazy Lop.
Slowly trotting around the course,
Eating grass, fruit and veg
Filing his hooves on the window ledge.

Max, Max, there's no horse like Max.
They say that he trots after cats.
He has a girlfriend just like him,
She's so disgusting she eats out of the bin.

Hayley Chisholm (9)
Hurst Green Primary School

MILLENNIUM IS HERE

Time for a change and a new beginning.
Drink all night and dance all day.
Party in the streets of London.
Millennium is here and it's here to stay.
Year 2000 is here with the millennium
And it will be here forever.

Charlotte Preston (9)
Hurst Green Primary School

RAIN

I target an umbrella,
I make it wet with a splash.
I land on a hot tin roof.
Then I turn into water vapour.
I need to be careful when I land,
even in some Diet Coke.
Sometimes I land on awkward people,
then I give them a soak.

People get wet because of me,
They don't like me one bit,
I wish I could do something else.
I quit!

I'm taking a holiday, I've had enough.
I'm going up to Heaven
but I'm sick of going there,
so I think I'll go to Devon.

Lee Oakley (8)
Joseph Turner Primary School

WHO IS THAT IN THE MIRROR?

Who is that in the mirror
with browny-blond hair
so wispy and curly?
His ears are small,
with his hair tucked behind.
With one ear pierced.

Who is that in the mirror?
His eyes are green as emeralds.
His eyelashes long and black.
His eyebrows thin and wispy.

Who is that in the mirror
with moles all over?
His nose round and big.
His mouth is big and straight
and his lips big and bold.

Tell me, who is that in the mirror?

Why, is it me?

Mark Roper (9)
Joseph Turner Primary School

WHAT AM I?

I struck a tree, set it on fire.
I made a bang in the sky turned it blue.
I knocked an aerial off the top of a roof.
I made the rain come which made me stop!
Goodbye from me.
(At least for now).

Lucy Moore (8)
Joseph Turner Primary School

THE HOUSE CAT

The house cat is big and fat.
He likes to rip curtains.
He has sharp claws.
He's vicious and strong.
Sometimes he is happy.
Sometimes he can jump as high
                    as an elephant.
He has got straight whiskers.
He is a brown cat.
Sometimes he is naughty.

Nathan Osborne (8)
Joseph Turner Primary School

MYSELF

My hair is short
and it is brown.
My eyes are big.
My nose is small
and my ears stick out.
My cheeks are red.
I have a mole by my top lip
and my bottom lip is fat
and my head is like an egg shape.

Adam Scott (9)
Joseph Turner Primary School

HURRICANE

I blew a tree branch off a palm tree
and flattened it right into the ground.
I blew roofs off houses and blew cars into trees.
I blew shops onto motorways and crashed into hills.
I blew fences into tents and caravans.
Then all of a sudden I went into a gentle breeze
that blew me into the sea.
Help!
   Help!
      Help!
         Help!
            Help!

Gemma Jones (8)
Joseph Turner Primary School

HURRICANE

I pulled a tree out of the undergrowth
and tore it to smithereens.
I blew a caravan into a hotel.
I blew a hotel on to the M6 motorway.
I blew a tent into a person
and knocked him flat.
Then the tide carried me back out to sea.

Johnathon Shelton (9)
Joseph Turner Primary School

THE TABBY CAT

Glowing eyes in the alleys.
Sharp claws sparking in the darkness.
Tail spinning behind him.
Fur swaying in the wind.
Thin ears sticking up in the sky.
He pounces on the mice!
Vicious teeth eating.

Richard Rudge (8)
Joseph Turner Primary School

THE STREET CAT

The street cat's a little bit fat.
The tabby cat lives in the trash.
They live in a flat with lots of cats
that visit the flat.
Smelly, smelly cats.

Gemma Perry (8)
Joseph Turner Primary School

THE ALLEY CAT

The alley cat is Sally.
She's a bit *fatty*.
Lives in `a *flattie*.
With *fatty* friends.
She's got *clattie* claws,
Clattie, clattie, clattie!
Across the windows.
She's a mad cat.

Lucy Howes (8)
Joseph Turner Primary School

ROSIE THE CAT

I have a cat named Rosie.
She has green, glowing eyes.
When you turn the light off her eyes glow green.
She is a tortoiseshell.
She is fat and she goes through the cat flap.
She is very furry.
She is a small cat and she is a good cat.
She likes to lie on her blanket.
She is great fun to play with
and she goes to sleep on my bed.
When I wake up she jumps.

Amy Bastable (8)
Joseph Turner Primary School

TORNADO

I rip houses out of the ground.
I swish them round and round.
I throw them a mile
and it takes an hour to land.
They land, windows smashed,
doors hanging off,
in the middle of the ocean.

Ritchie Walton (8)
Joseph Turner Primary School

SUN

I rise from behind the clouds in the early morning.
I light up the world to give it light.
I give the Earth a lot of heat to keep it warm.
I'm made of fire that is really hot.
I can kill people.
I'm out in space.
I sleep behind the clouds.
It's getting really dark.
So goodnight.

Mitchell Davis (8)
Joseph Turner Primary School

SNOW

I come down, down, down and down,
I am made up of frozen water.
Children come out to play
then they build snowmen and throw snowballs.
I come down on roads and pavements,
then I do most damage, like making people and cars slip.
I am tired now,
I have to go.

Jastinder Samra (9)
Joseph Turner Primary School

THUNDER AND LIGHTNING

I'm crashing every now and again.
Hitting the ground like a thunderbolt.
Making such a *bang!*
I feel like a giant
shaking the ground.
I light up the Earth.
I think I'm the king of the Earth and space.
I destroy flowers, trees and plants.
I make fences fall down with my strength.
I flash at night-time like a torch.

What am I?

Heather Summers (8)
Joseph Turner Primary School

RAIN

I am wet and see-through too.
I can wet your washing.
I can get you wet,
so I'd watch out if I were you!

Shaun Barratt (9)
Joseph Turner Primary School

WHAT AM I?

With flashes of light
and as quick as a tick
I come from the heavens
and usually come at night.

I come as a streak,
I can be yellow
and I make people shriek
and they can't put their head on the pillow.

I strike a bird and see its bones.
I am losing my power.
I'm going back up to the heavens.
Can you guess what I am?

Mitchell Green (8)
Joseph Turner Primary School

THE CHILD

Raggy, raggy
with untied laces.
Dragging around
in different places.
Hangin' out shirt
an' covered in dirt.
This is the look
of the child.

Caroline Adams (9)
Langley Primary School

LOVE IS IN THE AIR

Love is in the air, or is it just a joke?
But
Can it bring you to buying a loved one flowers?
Can you end up having a date?
Is love romantic?
Is love passionate?
Can love bring you to having a candlelit dinner at the Ritz Café?
Can you end up kissing in the dim light?
Can you end up getting engaged.
Then does it bring you to getting married?
Is that what love is all about?

Marie Adkins (9)
Langley Primary School

MARY I

Mary, Mary a devoted Catholic,
to be a Protestant or Catholic she had to pick.
Burn, burn, never kind,
she had to leave her past behind.

Married, married tried to have a kid,
Philip left, that was his bid.
Childless, childless, broken-hearted,
to her funeral she was carted.

Helen Skett (9)
Langley Primary School

MONSTERS

There once was a monster called Mikey,
He was very big and spiky.
He was deep, deep blue and covered with gue
And came from the planet Zikey.

There once was a monster called Dotty,
She was very small and spotty.
She had a friend called Josie who was very nosy
And had hair which was really knotty.

There once was a monster called Ink,
Who was very kind and pink.
She never moaned, she never groaned
And she fitted into a sink!

Anneka Davis (9)
Langley Primary School

SNOW

Snow! Snow
Let it come
Glitter, bitter.
Heavy or light.
Please! Please!
Let it come.
Haily or icy.
Please! Please!
Let it come.
Just let it come.

Manwinder Kaur Gosal (9)
Langley Primary School

THE ORPHAN

Life as an orphan,
Roaming the streets,
No presents
No treats,
Unhappy face,
People stare in disgrace,
You have no shoes,
You have no socks.
Smiling children
With golden locks,
Stare on in disgrace
At your despicable face
Yet there is no difference
Between them and you.

Amanda Thomson (9)
Langley Primary School

MY FRIEND

I have a friend called Polly,
She's very, very jolly.
She giggles and she titters,
She chuckles and she sniggers.
So now I've gone off with Dolly.

Now I'm friends with Dolly,
I've found out she's like Polly.
She giggles and she titters,
She chuckles and she sniggers.
I really hate people so jolly.

Alisha Davis (9)
Langley Primary School

THE ENCHANTING BOX

I will put in the box:

The sparkling grass,
fire from the hairband,
Yasmin my friend who will always help me.

I will put in the box:

My dog Tyson
and a poster of Boyzone.

I will put in the box:

My sister Alicia with her cheesy smile.
A book of the Spice Girls.

My box is made of sparkling stars
and the lid has got sky dancers on it.

Jodie Austin (9)
Langley Primary School

THE DIRTY CORNER

In my horrible corner, I'd place:
Old stinky mushrooms.
mushy peas,
white creamy milk.

In my horrible corner, I'd dump:
Getting up,
cleaning my bedroom,
doing my history work.

In my horrible corner, I'd shove:
Creepy-crawly spiders,
people taking my friends away,
snakes slithering.

In my horrible corner, I'd chuck:
Yucky, bucky raisins,
the colour brown,
pure red tomatoes.

Poonam Khosla (9)
Langley Primary School

MY HORRID CORNER

In my horrid corner I'd lob:
Getting out of bed.
Glasses on my face
and writing.

In my horrid corner, I'd place:
Dancing.
Turning off the TV
and poems.

In my horrid corner, I'd toss:
Wet playtimes.
School.
Spinach.

In my horrid corner, I'd kick:
Stories.
Tidying up my bedroom
and geography.

Ranveer Purewal (8)
Langley Primary School

THE MAGICAL BOX!

I will put in the box:

The most colourful pens ever.
The first roar of a lion cub.
The joey in a kangaroo's pouch.

I will put in the box:

The fluffy wool from a sheep
All the colours from an angel fish.
The first man on the moon.
The tooth from a great white shark.

My box is made of gold and silver
With fireworks on the lid
And surprises in the corners.

I will become an artist in my box
And draw a masterpiece.

Luke Condley (9)
Langley Primary School

THE GRUESOME CORNER

In my gruesome corner, I'd put:
My horrible keyboard
and getting out of bed
and packing for my holiday.

In my gruesome corner, I'd kick:
January.
Going up hills on horses
and drawing.

In my gruesome corner, I'd push:
The rain.
Going to my cousin's house
and going to bed.

Kelly Ann Averall (8)
Langley Primary School

'QUACK' SAID THE BILLY GOAT

'Quack!' said the billy goat.
'Oink!' said the hen.
'Miaow!' said the little chick,
running in the pen!

'Gobble-gobble!' said the dog.
'Cluck!' said the sow.
'Tu-whit-tu-whoo!' the donkey cried.
'Baa!' said the cow!

'Hee-haw!' the turkey said.
The duck began to moo!
All at once the sheep
went, 'Cock-a-doodle-doo!'

The owl coughed and cleared his throat
and he began to moo.
'Bow-wow!' said the cock,
swimming in a loo!

'Cheep-cheep!' said the cat,
as she began to fly !
Farmer's been and laid an egg,
that's the reason why!

Gurpreet Sukhain (9)
Langley Primary School

THE MAGICAL BOX

I will put in the box:

A bright sun on a summer's day
And ten golden daffodils.
A large chocolate ice-cream
And a large dark-blue sea.
The first *neigh* from a horse.

I will put in the box:

A scrumptious basket of sweets
And a sparkling diamond.
The first bark of a dog
A golden pretty dress
And a first miaow of a cat.

My box is fashioned.
It is dark purple.
We see yellow, golden stars
With hinges from ducks' toes.

I shall skate in my box
On the high, cold winds
Till the sun rises high
And I can see the colours of the sky.

Keshia Bailey (9)
Langley Primary School

MY HORRIBLE CORNER

In my horrible corner I'd place:
Nits.
Raining when I can't go out.
Snow.

In my horrible corner I'd chuck:
Mushy peas.
Sitting by a boy.
A football in my face.

In my horrible corner I'd throw:
Tidying up.
Stepping on hard pebbles.
Creepy caterpillars.

In my horrible corner I'd shove:
Spiders,
Brown bread.
Hard words.

Kerry Pugh (9)
Langley Primary School

THE HORRIBLE CORNER

In my horrible corner I'd shove:
Mushrooms.
Getting up.
Doing the washing up.

In my horrible corner I'd drop:
Tomato soup.
Creepy spiders.
Doing work at school.

In my horrible corner I'd dump:
Someone taking my friend away.
Somebody kicking the ball in my face.
Going to pubs.

In my horrible corner I'd chuck:
Dead flowers.
Tidying up my bedroom.
Dead rats.

Kavita Prashar (9)
Langley Primary School

CRICKET

The dust flows as the batsman runs
A ball ready to be caught from the air
Bounce from the bowler's bowl
The white rope round the circle ground.

The wickets are standing ready to be hit
Colourful kits on the players brighten the game up
Glasses they wear from the bursting sun
And also the umpire who rules the game.

Chris Kelleher (9)
Lapal Primary School

COLOURS, COLOURS EVERYWHERE

Colours, colours everywhere,
Bright, dark, cool and warm,
Colours, colours everywhere,
Dull, light, calm and vibrant.

Blue is the calm sea,
The bluebells swaying around,
The bright blue sky and,
The bluebird flying and not making a sound.

Yellow are the sunflowers waiting for the rain,
The sun is shining brightly,
Whilst Laa-Laa's shouting, 'Again, again!'
And the sand glistens in the light.

Red is danger,
Po is here,
The tulips have opened and
Valentine's Day is here for this one time of the year.

Silver is the frost still on the ground,
The stars are up in the night sky,
A cold winter's morning and
The icicles are hanging high.

Orange is fresh oranges,
The flames are alight,
The sun is setting and
The indicators are bright.

Green is the grass blowing in the wind,
Dipsy is saying, 'Eh oh!'
The frogs are leaping about and
The leaves in the forest have fallen low.

Claire Dunn (9)
Lapal Primary School

MY CAT

He sits in the garden on a warm summer's day,
Until the time is right when he jumps upon his prey.
He's sleek and elegant and his paws don't make a sound,
As he runs through the garden and lands on the ground.
A delicious morsel would be a bird sitting high upon a branch,
If the bird swooped down he'd jump up high and catch it by chance.
The garden is a jungle just waiting to be explored,
It's easy finding a cat just look where it's clawed.

Alex Penrose (9)
Lapal Primary School

FOOTBALL

F   ootball players get lots of money when they play well.
O   n the side of the pitch is where the manager sits.
O   n every weekday morning teams do training.
T   eams who are good win the cups.
B   rilliant teams get good stadiums.
A   lot of people support their favourite teams.
L   ong painted lines mark the pitch.
L   ots of teams have good players.

David Kelleher (9)
Lapal Primary School

THE ELEPHANT

As it charges through the jungle
When it has bellyache
Other animals go barmy
As if it is a race.
The floor shakes
The trees fall down
Guess who it is?

The elephant.

Timothy Seymour (9)
Lapal Primary School

DOWN BY THE RIVER

We walked along the river,
The water is smooth as can be.
The birds sing so lovely
And the daffodils are so pretty.
The boats go past me
And the people on the boat wave to me.
The sun is very shiny
And there are birds flying past me
And there is a boat going into the lock
And the grass is as green as can be.

Jack Johnson (7)
Leighswood School

DOWN BY THE RIVER

We walked along the river
It was a lot of fun.
It was peaceful.
There were narrowboats sailing along,
The sun was gleaming on.
The river was reflecting on me.
We walked along the river bank.

Jack Pemberton (7)
Leighswood School

CONCENTRATING

When Philippa's in her room
Perming her hair.
We like to help her concentrate
By shouting, *'Err, er, er!'*

Charlotte Bodin (7)
Leighswood School

BARONESS JUGULA

The walls were closing in as I went deeper into her garden.
I was terrified out of my wits.
She had five-headed snakes,
She had a swamp.
She had thorns and spiky bushes.
She had a half bull and half tiger.
She had wolves that bit at my heels.
She had a bear that roared like mad.

Then I came to the door where I paused and knocked.
Then this ugly creature came out of the door.
Baroness Jugula:
Then I remembered what I came for,
'Are you ready for me to refurbish your house yet?'

Katie Mulvey (9)
Maney Hill Primary School

HARRY THE CAT

Harry the cat
Is kind of fat,
He's got a long tail,
And sleeps on the mat!

He's quick and eager,
And climbs up trees,
And likes to play with fallen leaves.

He goes out to play,
And chases mice,
He bring them home
But that's not nice.

He drinks his milk,
And likes some fuss,
When I call him in,
I shout,
'Puss, Puss!'

Matthew Hathaway (9)
Maney Hill Primary School

COLOURS

I like colours,
because they're bright.
I like pink,
because it makes me think.
I like lime green,
because it's not mean.
I like blue,
because it's so true.
I like red
because it's on the sheet on my bed.
I like brown,
because it doesn't make me frown.
But my favourite colour of all the rest is orange,
I love orange the best!

Gagandeep Degun (9)
Maney Hill Primary School

OUT OF MY WINDOW

Out of my window
Something appeared,
I didn't know what it was
which came through the window.

I went to the window, I had a little peep
and saw what it was.
I looked in amazement.
I thought I was dreaming
I didn't really know.

I thought it was a fairy boy named Link
and he was kind, I think.
He had a sword and quite a big shield
I said, 'Goodnight,' and he disappeared.

Christopher Littler (8)
Maney Hill Primary School

INTO THE LAIR OF BARONESS JUGULA

Summer never falls on the grounds of the lair
The gardens there are mostly bare
Dreadful things like skulls are there
Everything would give you a scare.
Leaves fall off an ancient oak tree
Each one landing with a thud
Bloodcurdling shrieks come from a derelict allotment.
In the night fearsome foxes hunt their prey
Spiders spin their webs between eyeholes in a skull
Poisonous foliage dangles off a hedge
And fierce piranhas swim in a pool
Slithery snakes squirm back and forth,
And evil hawks nibble a dead rabbit
And blood drips off a skull
And troublesome hyenas run about
In the dead of night;
And drooping flowers collapse on the ground,
And flesh dangles off an ancient bone.
I got to the door and rattled the knocker
It echoed;
The door opened
And the horrible face of Baroness Jugula appeared.
Then I remembered why I'd come
'Can I interest you in UPVC windows?'

James Barrell (9)
Maney Hill Primary School

THE SCREAMING CAT

The screaming cat
Screams at the top of the castle
The screaming cat
Screams at the top of his voice.

Sharp claws and fangs
Monster's yellow eyes
Who haunts the towers of Tamworth Castle
Who haunts the towers, dungeons . . .

The ghosts of his ancestors rise from the dead to haunt the living
The screaming cat is behind this door
I opened the door with a squeak
But the screaming cat is only a
Kitten!

Morgan Davison (9)
Maney Hill Primary School

LEAVES

There are leaves flowing slowly in the sky,
Leaves crackling in the air,
Slowly crunching.
Red, yellow, orange, brown
Coloured leaves.
Raining leaves,
Falling, twinkling leaves.
Down,
Down,
Down,
Crunching leaves,
Red crackling leaves.

Aaron Griffin (7)
Mount Pleasant Primary School

POLAR BEAR

Nothing to do,
Nothing to see,
Only a little polar bear,
Twirling, glittering,
Gazing, sprinkling,
Scattering,
Polar bear,
Crystal, sparkly eyes,
He's slipping on the snow,
Sliding gracefully.

Jemma Worsfold (8)
Mount Pleasant Primary School

LEAVES

There are leaves falling, floating,
There are leaves like a quilt on the ground,
The colours - brown, gold, crimson,
Feeling crunchy, crumpled and rough.

Down,
Down,
Down,
Slowly fall the leaves.

Sophia Mifsud (8)
Mount Pleasant Primary School

THE WINTER POEM

The snow dazzles in the air,
The icicles so misty and the air so powdery,
The snowflake so twirly,
The icicles so frozen and twinkling in the air,
But, oh no, the sun has returned!
Goodbye.

Grace Zentilin (8)
Mount Pleasant Primary School

LEAVES

Floating leaves drifting down
On the ground, then we hear
Crunchy, golden leaves, crunchy, golden leaves,
And crimson leaves dancing in the air,
Lovely golden leaves crackling in the sky,
So wonderful, creamy leaves.

Luke Dawes (7)
Mount Pleasant Primary School

LEAVES

I see the golden quilt,
And the quilt can keep the ground warm,
The quilt is like a fire in leaves,
And the fire turns into the leaves,
Now it turns into golden dust.

Steve Dunn (7)
Mount Pleasant Primary School

80

THE FIRST SNOW

One day, the snow came knocking on my door,
It went and covered the rooftops and the floor
With its twinkling white fur coat,
Leaving a beautiful white, snowy scene,
Whizzing east, west, north and south,
Now it's disappearing, I hope the sun never comes.

Danielle Smith (7)
Mount Pleasant Primary School

SNOWFLAKES

Snowflakes, snowflakes glittering in the air,
Falling, falling, falling out of nowhere,
Snow falls onto the ground,
Sugar is on the rivers.

Jade Ross (7)
Mount Pleasant Primary School

SNOW

The snow has come,
It's knocking on my roof and door,
I watch it coming, snow, snow, will it come again?
If it does, *snow fight!*

Daniel Meredith (7)
Mount Pleasant Primary School

WINTER SNOW

Sprinkling snow covers the misty air,
Cold like scattering pieces of ice.
Powdery frost comes, like diamonds and crystal dots.
Everything is lovely,
It's twirling,
Glittering,
Gliding with snow.
I think it will be a whizzing wonder.
Full world tonight.

Jennifer Simmonds (7)
Mount Pleasant Primary School

LEAVES

Leaves cover the ground with a quilty quilt, tumble like a leaf,
Crimsony, red, yellow leaves are like a fire,
Crumbling, crunchy leaves crumble on the ground,
Cover the ground with a soft quilt, colours like a fire,
Leaves are colourful like orange paint,
Leaves dance like fire,
Leaves are rough and crunchy, like magic carpets falling on the ground,
Leaves are crunchy like a crackling fire.

Daniel Homer (8)
Mount Pleasant Primary School

LEAVES

I see leaves falling down,
Their creamy, fiery leaves floating,
I hear crunchy, rough, wrinkled, chattering leaves,
I feel wonderful, goldy, fire-dancing leaves,
I hear crackling, golden, scampering, leaf mice,
Dancing, crumpled, crunchy, frolicking, crimson,
Dancing leaves.

Gabriella Zentilin (8)
Mount Pleasant Primary School

LEAVES

Leaves flow golden and brown,
Like a rainbow covering the leaves in autumn,
The leaves dancing around.
Autumn is the best time of the year,
It's quiet when the leaves whoosh around.

Matthew Simonian (7)
Mount Pleasant Primary School

LEAVES

I can see crumpled leaves falling down like a quilt on the ground,
They remind me of a big fire heating up,
Golden, crimson, yellow, brown and green.

They remind me of little men scampering around,
I can see leaves dancing in the air
In a big circle up around my head.

Jamie Checketts (7)
Mount Pleasant Primary School

LEAVES

Leaves floating, dancing in the sky, their golden beauty of their
Colour, creamy, crunchy, crumpled up on the ground like a quilt,
Dancing is their favourite thing to do, the lovely colour of the
Leaves themselves, fire is their colour, on the window they
Stand crumpled, scampering about, like mice whirling about,
The wonderful smell of mint in the air,
The golden dust flashing about,
Then there they lie, still on the ground.

Kelly Parton (8)
Mount Pleasant Primary School

LEAVES

I see the leaves floating along with the wind,
Dancing along with the wind,
I hear them crackling,
They feel hard and stiff,
I think they're magic, but they are not,
When they hit the ground it goes crack.

Paul Godwin (8)
Mount Pleasant Primary School

LEAVES

I see floating leaves like a blanket,
The colours I see are; gold, crimson, fiery,
crunchy, creamy like the fire,
Burning like a hot, sunny day,
I feel like I could
Just stand in the grass.

Lewis Mason (7)
Mount Pleasant Primary School

LEAVES

Falling leaves flutter about in the sky,
Their colours are creamy, golden too,
I hear rough noises in the sky,
I see the leaves dancing in the sky together,
I feel the warm leaves are making me a quilt,
Leaves are sweet, like a bird.

Holly Taylor (7)
Mount Pleasant Primary School

LEAVES

The leaves fall from the sky,
And they fly so high, so slowly
Falling on the ground,
Then they make the sound
Of crunching.

Stefan Davies (7)
Mount Pleasant Primary School

LEAVES

I can see a tree with lovely leaves,
The colours of the leaves are crimson and brown,
I can hear a crumple and a swishing,
I can feel a blanket on the ground.

Daniel Orford (7)
Mount Pleasant Primary School

AQUA

Smoothly, silently, the sea glistened,
Lonely the sea lay, everybody listened,
Blue, green, turquoise and white,
Now the sea and sky together combine,
The sea is aqua, blue and green,
The most glistening sight I've ever seen,
The moon is brightly shining,
On the sea it's hiding,
All the people go to bed,
The sea stays outside instead,
Now the stars are shining bright,
Now the sky is pitch black.

Olivia Hammond (9)
Mount Pleasant Primary School

HAVE YOU SEEN A LITTLE DOG?

Have you see a little dog anywhere about?
A raggy dog, a shaggy dog, who's always looking out
For some fresh mischief which he thinks he really ought to do.
He's very likely at this minute to be biting someone's shoe.

Lloyd A Rose (9)
Mount Pleasant Primary School

VICTORIAN TIMES

In Victorian times the sky was dark,
Then you would hear the dogs all bark.

Nailmakers getting little pay,
As they work hard all day.

The Round Oak working and making iron and steel,
And chainmakers, hot, that's how they feel.
Glassmaking from Brierley Hill,
Mines inside are cold and chill.

Thomas Mullard (9)
Mount Pleasant Primary School

THE LISTENERS

He quietly knocked,
But the door was locked,
No one was there,
Something sounding like a bear,
The traveller crawled through the door,
And he shouted, but it echoed even more,
The phantom stood still,
By an old house by the mill.

Christopher Griffin (9)
Mount Pleasant Primary School

THE ARRIVAL

The cottage stood eerie and silent,
The moonlight cast shadows so strange,
He approached on silent footsteps,
He smelt smoke, there's a fire in the range.

He tapped and the door creaked inwards,
The air cold as ice and tainted with fear,
Not a sound could be heard, not a whisper,
He stepped in, the stranger was *here!*

Emma Jane Layland (9)
Mount Pleasant Primary School

GRAPES

I like grapes,
Grapes like me,
I eat grapes
For my tea,
I eat grapes
For my lunch,
It's so great,
I can eat a
Whole bunch.

Natalie McDonald (9)
Mount Pleasant Primary School

COLUMBUS

Columbus, a man, bold yet sincere,
He set off going West, knowing no fear.
Columbus, determined hero and brave,
His aim was gold and lots of slaves.
Columbus, proud, an elegant sight,
The fear of thirst night after night.
Columbus a courageous, skilful man,
To arrive at the Indies was his plan.
Columbus' adventure, a great success,
He claimed the islands for Spain to possess.

Michael J North (9)
Mount Pleasant Primary School

VIKINGS!

A fearsome dragon fiend from the mist,
Advancing with sails as red as blood,
Tumultuous cries, swords clanging,
Creaking oars, splashing in the foaming ocean,
Dark waters, erupting with power, energy and might,
Warriors leaping from their ships,
Roars! Battle cries and shouts!

Vikings Victorious!

Charlotte Elise Harris (9)
Mount Pleasant Primary School

THE PIKEMAN

His name is Simon
and he is the pikeman,
I fight people in close hand,
what a fine ship I was working on
I was in my cabin
when it started sinking,
I got up and started thinking,
What was happening?
So I went up to have.a quick look,
and I was under the water and drowning.
The Mary Rose was such a story,
and in the end it had no glory.

David Clarke (9)
Mount Pleasant Primary School

THE LISTENERS

A traveller knocked upon a door,
and a ghostly shudder came upon the floor.
In a puff of smoke he had gone,
he was as scared as everyone.
Up on the turret he would go,
then his face would really glow.
But he had an escape plan,
and soon he ran and ran.

Iain Geddes (8)
Mount Pleasant Primary School

WILLIAM THE CARPENTER

Name: William Carpenter,
I am the carpenter
That makes and mends
On the Mary Rose
Which never ends
Until 1545,
When hardly anyone survived,
And when she sank
She fell like a tank,
And when the water came in
It flooded my cabin,
And that's the sad story
Of when the Mary Rose had no glory.

Harry Williams (9)
Mount Pleasant Primary School

THE YELLOW SUNFLOWERS

The yellow sunflowers have grown so tall,
They peep right over the garden wall,
I wonder and wonder what they can see,
For the yellow sunflowers are taller than me.

Richard Bloomer (9)
Mount Pleasant Primary School

MILLENNIUM

It's the millennium so let's have a party party party,
it will be great great great, and
may be some champagne champagne champagne,
because it's the millennium,

It's the millennium so let's
have a dress up party party party,
then it will be great great great,
because it's the millennium,
and you know it is.

Lucy Foster (9)
Peters Hill Primary School

MILLENNIUM

M erry as we are driving along
I   n some time we find a space
L arge, no space at all
L ovely to see
E normous, absolutely
N ew year
N ew century, it's coming
I   lluminating bright sparks, here and there
U nforgetable, absolutely breathtaking
M illennium 2000, it's here, it's everywhere.

Richa Okhandiar (9)
Peters Hill Primary School

THE MILLENNIUM 2000

The millennium is nearly over now,
It will be the year 2000,
People will celebrate too.

I'll be 10 before millennium comes,
I'll bet we will go to a town hall,
1000 years are nearly over now.

Everybody is getting ready now,
The millennium is nearly here now,
The millennium has been waiting 1000 years.

Make this millennium the best day in your life,
Piles of new buildings are being built,
I'll drink piles of drink millennium night.

I hope everyone has a lovely time,
I hope we can stay up late like after midnight,
I am getting really excited now.

Say goodbye to the old millennium,
And say hello to the new millennium,
I hope it's going to be nice.

Michelle Cartwright (9)
Peters Hill Primary School

MILLENNIUM

The millennium.
Katie, what is the millennium?
An animal?
Stupid girl.
Sabrina, do you know?
No Miss.
Right.
John,
The same, John.
A place where melons grow?
Stupid.
The year 2000 class!
Oh, hello Miss Songia.
How nice! But what is the millennium?
I'm surrounded by idiots.
What is happening?
Miss, you're going crazy again.

Adèle James (9)
Peters Hill Primary School

MILLENNIUM 2000!

The year is over and now is the millennium.
2000!
New things, new homes, new places and new people.
2000!
In the millennium there will be the biggest party ever in our lifetime.
2000!
People will celebrate this day all over the world.
2000!
This all means our lives will be split over two centuries,
In the 2000!

Rebecca Glazzard (9)
Peters Hill Primary School

THE MILLENNIUM

I think that the new millennium will be great,
There could be robots to do your bed and things like that.

There could be great looking shoes that make a noise, bring, bring
There could be computers that can get your library books for you.

There could be time machines where you can look to the future,
There could be electric pens.

I wish there would be toys that did crazy things,
And things that did your work.

The millennium will be great!
Waahoo!

Jessica Calladine (9)
Peters Hill Primary School

THE MILLENNIUM

Say hello to the new century
    1000 years have gone by
The Millennium Dome is being built
    some say it's going to be
        really high
Aeroplanes are streaming by with banners
    tied to their tails,
You wait till millennium night
    fireworks with sparks will
Shimmer in the sky
    once again say hello to the new
Say goodbye to the old.

Emma Leddington (9)
Peters Hill Primary School

MILLENNIUM NONSENSE

In the millennium
I hope we don't have to come to
school, or fly to the moon in
a great big balloon.
Flying cars and bikes and folk
and babies that think it's all
a big joke. Coloured insects
that can destroy our town,
zooming up and down and
round and round.

We'll have jet-powered pens
and dens in the sky while
kids about ten sit and eat
chocolate pie.
Toys that come to life at
night and people having
strange fantasy flights.
Although this sounds silly
will it happen, - really?

Did I mention our trips
round the sun? All together
in a blackcurrant bun?
With holidays in space for
one and each with bright
orange suncream on Jupiter's beach.

I can't wait for the new millennium,
it won't be long, with new videos, TV, and
music and song,
enjoy this time with each
sister and brother,
for you can be sure you
won't see another!

Danielle Pearson (9)
Peters Hill Primary School

MILLENNIUM POEM

A thousand years is over,
A brand new start in life,
There will be party poppers everywhere,
Just for the
Millennium!

I can't wait for the millennium,
I'll be up till 12 o'clock,
I'll be having a drop of wine,
There will be balloons everywhere,
Just for the
Millennium!

It will be the year 2000
I'll be ten in that year,
When Big Ben hits 12 o'clock
There will be huge parties,
Just for the
Millennium!

Thomas Hampton (9)
Peters Hill Primary School

MILLENNIUM

The millennium is going to be a great time,
Time for a new teacher,
Say goodbye to the old person,
And say *hello* to the new person.

Flying around in solar powered cars,
And lots, lots more,
As well as solar-powered cars,
You can have jet-powered pens.

What about in the year 3000,
More things to do,
I just can't wait till the year 2000.

In the year 2000,
I want flash cars and more sweets,
But remember you still have to go to school,
Stay up really late and join in the wild crowd,
It's the millennium.

Jonathan Siebert (9)
Peters Hill Primary School

THE YEAR 2000!

The millennium is another 1000 years,
I hope we can fly,
Fly to the moon or even the sun,
We would have fun . . .

The millennium is another 1000 years,
No more school,
No more work,
Just stay at home and watch the Millennium Dome . . .

The millennium is another 1000 years,
New buildings are being built,
Lots of people are celebrating,
I can't wait till the millennium,
Can you?

Beth Lucas (9)
Peters Hill Primary School

MILLENNIUM POEM

Hooray, hooray, alleluia,
It's a new year,
Hooray, hooray, alleluia,
It's the millennium.

Come on Mum, come on Mum,
It's a new year,
Come on Mum, come on Mum,
It's the millennium.

Drinks, fireworks, presents,
It's a new century,
Drinks, fireworks, presents,
It's a new century.

It's the millennium,
The millennium,

The

Millennium.

Lauren Jasper (9)
Peters Hill Primary School

THE MILLENNIUM

T he millennium is approaching fast.
H undreds of people in the streets.
E very one of them smiling happily.

M ums and dads buying food.
I n the house cooking is . . .
L illy the cook making soup.
L oads of people come to the great feast.
E ven the president of England.
N an looks after the baby.
N obody hears the baby crying all over the chatting.
I   think they enjoyed themselves.
U ncle Fred has gone to bed
M um and Dad see everyone out.

Christopher Del-Vecchio (9)
Peters Hill Primary School

MILLENNIUM

The millennium is nearly here.
Men are drinking lots of beer.
Ladies are flying round in ships to
Find a bag of gorgeous chips.
I'm really excited, I'm really glad
So are my mum and dad.
For the millennium I'm going to get
A brand-new pet.
Not a hamster, not a horse,
Not a hog, but a dog of course.
The millennium is nearly here,
So let's give a great big *cheer!*

Megan Dobson (9)
Peters Hill Primary School

MILLENNIUM

What will happen in the year 2000?
Will there be food processors to produce food
Or could there be digital television so people will never be bored?
Will there be new computers so people can learn more?

What will happen in the year 2000?
Will there be a new Prime Minister or King or Queen,
Or will they discover if there is life on Mars?

What will happen in the year 2000?
Will the Millennium Dome be built,
Or will they be able to make the space station up in space?

What will happen in the year 2000?

Nobody knows!

Andrew Stevens (9)
Peters Hill Primary School

THE MILLENNIUM

The millennium is a new year,
don't shed a tear!
The millennium is a fun place to be,
so hurry, hurry to see!
The millennium is a party time,
so don't waste your time!
The millennium is going to be history,
and in a couple, it will be a big mystery!
The millennium is a new decade, century and all,
so when it's the millennium I'll be quite tall!

Katherine Tromans (9)
Peters Hill Primary School

Year 2000

Millennium is a great time to celebrate with beer and wine,
People dance about with joy and glee
Nearly everybody sings the Auld Lang Syne song
By Robert Burns the poem writer.

It's going to be cool,
When it turns 12 o'clock, it will be the millennium,
Millennium, millennium, millennium!

But people say inventions will be made,
Also new stars will be made,
You never know a comet might hit the world.

Football stars, tennis stars, new winners in the world,
New plans for school,
New teachers will be made,
So roll up everybody here it comes.

Millennium is here!

Gregory Allen (9)
Peters Hill Primary School

Millennium

It's here, at last,
1999 is in the past.
Come over here and drink some beer,
It's a new millennium.

Come on have fun,
I hope there will be lots of sun.
Stand up, make a toast,
A new show I might host.
It's a new millennium.

It's come, then gone,
A new light has shone,
It's now the year 2001,
The new millennium has gone.

Matthew Sidaway (9)
Peters Hill Primary School

MILLENNIUM

It's come, it's come!
It's time for the millennium
People are shouting
It's the *millennium!*

And people thought we would be in spaceships,
Tut
We are just the same as before.

I wish it was time now for the year 2000!
I wish, I wish, I wish,
I really do *wish!*

I wonder what the year 3000 will be like?
Maybe it will be the same?
I really wonder.

Ben Holdaway (9)
Peters Hill Primary School

My Bedroom

My bedroom has been painted,
When Nat came in she fainted.
There was nothing I could do,
I think she caught the flu.

Her mummy took her home,
She washed her face with foam.
My bedroom must be bright,
Though the yellow is quite light.

One of the colours is green,
The green looks quite mean.
Another wall is blue,
It's really quite true.

The other one is yellow,
It could make you bellow!
My bedroom has been painted,
When Nat came in she fainted.

Louise Hickman (9)
St John's CE JMI School, Walsall Wood

School

I enjoy going to school
Because the teachers are cool
When the bell rings
We all go into assembly and start to sing.

At dinner time we all look around
We don't make a sound
We all start to talk
Then we all go to class and work.

Mandeep Kaur (9)
St John's CE JMI School, Walsall Wood

THE TROUT AND THE CROC

The trout and the croc went swimming one day
Under the ponds and far away.
The trout and the croc went hunting one day
Over the banks and far one day.

They went to the dove, and asked for love
But the dove said get engaged.
So they got engaged and
Out came love.

Thanks to the dove
After a year they were a couple.
They had a baby boy, it was a trout
All it did was jump about.

Scott Bailey (9)
St John's CE JMI School, Walsall Wood

CHOCOLATE

Chocolate swirls around
Chocolate eaten in dozens
Chocolate . . . so tempting
Chocolate . . . so tasty
Chocolate tells you that it is delicious,
The chocolate says come and get me.
Chocolate is the best
Chocolate melts in your mouth
Chocolate has different tastes and different flavours.

Phillip Westwood (9)
St Mary's RC Primary School, Brierley Hill

ALL ABOUT DECLAN

Declan Greenway is the best,
Except the times when he's a pest.
Even though he has no hair,
We'll always know that he is there.

He has dark brown hair and dark brown eyes,
That glows in the dark at 5 o'clock.
The sound of the clock gives a chime.

Even though he'd kiss every girl in sight,
You might end up having a fight.
So you can pack your bags and go away,
But we'll be thinking of you every day.

Danial Williams
St Mary's RC Primary School, Brierley Hill

MRS CUTLER

There is a teacher from St Mary's School
She is quite a fool.

Her name is Mrs Cutler
She likes to mess with a big cooker.

She is always late,
She gets up at eight.

When she's at school,
She is very cool.

Gareth Jones (9)
St Mary's RC Primary School, Brierley Hill

JACKET POTATO

Lovely hot jacket potato
Coming out of the oven
Going on the dish
Your hands ready to grip the cheese,
Putting it on the potato like straw
The jacket potato steaming hot
Picking my knife and fork up
Ready to break the potato like ice
Into tiny ice cubes, then the best bit comes
Putting the potato cubes in your mouth
Yum, the cheese making a lovely taste
'Oh' it's all gone, that's the worst
Bit of all about a jacket potato.

Lucy O'Grady (9)
St Mary's RC Primary School, Brierley Hill

MEERKATS

M eerkats are my favourite
E xcellent they are,
E specially when they fall,
R ain is their favourite weather
K ats are my favourite, that's why I like them,
A nd they like to jump about all day long,
T heir eyes look like cats,
S oft and cuddly meerkats they are.

Natalie Fernihough (9)
St Mary's RC Primary School, Brierley Hill

SUMMER SUN

The summer sun increases as I walk outside,
I feel as if I'm in the oven.
The garden flowers are very colourful, they're very pretty too.
My baby sister splashes water from the paddling pool,
I feel my sweat trickle down my face.
Then I see my cousins, they are drinking a cool drink.
I beg and beg and beg for just a sip, they turn away in disgust.
My throat feels like a sandy desert. I'll never get a drink.
But then I see a drink of ice-cold coke. I feel like I've found treasure.
I run like a cheetah, I sip the Coke, I'm in Heaven, so for now goodbye!

Katie Pace (9)
St Mary's RC Primary School, Brierley Hill

THE BEST SUMMER EVER

Melting ice-cream on a hot day,
It was a glorious morning in May.
Lying on the beach,
Eating a juicy peach.
Playing in a sand pit,
Swimming in the salty sea,
Catching a faint tan.

Little children running about,
While people relax on the white sand.
Flying my kite in the sky,
It goes so very high.

Nicole Smith (9)
St Mary's RC Primary School, Brierley Hill

SPELLINGS, OH SPELLINGS

My spellings I hate them
Every week, every day.
'Do we have to do them?'
Every time I say.

She always says
'Yes you do Emma Russon,
Don't be a lazy girl.'
I hate school, why do they exist?

My spellings I don't learn them
I get them all wrong.
My mum shouts at me when I get them all wrong.
I get a smack before I go to bed.

My friend Nicola Kendrick,
She gets them all right.
I wish I was the same
As everybody else.

Stevie Read (9)
Woodlands Primary School

BIRTHDAYS ARE COMING

Birthdays are coming!
Birds are humming.
Hear people rapping
While rain is tapping.
See men drilling
As well as singing.
Birthdays are coming!

And mine's in May!

Lucy Fletcher (8)
Woodlands Primary School

THE BIG RACE

The hare and the tortoise had a race
But the hare had a very big pace
The bell to start went ding a ling a ling
You must run round in a ring
My hare thought he was clever
So he stopped altogether
But the tortoise carried on
We thought the hare had gone
He was fast asleep ·
In his dream he was counting sheep
The tortoise won
The hare woke up by the sun
He shouldn't have been clever from the start!

Stacey Oakley (9)
Woodlands Primary School

ANIMALS

There are brown ones
Black ones, white ones too
Thin ones, fat ones
Ones as big as you
Strong ones, weak ones
Fighting ones - some that do kung-fu
Long ones, short ones,
Loud ones, quiet ones in all they do
Scaly ones, furry ones
Mean ones, kind ones and some with goo!

Rachael Pope (9)
Woodlands Primary School

I LOVE LORRIES

I love lorries especially blue,
I don't fancy pink!
I love red lorries the colour of blood,
and I love green ones too!
I must not forget yellow the colour of a Weetabix box.
I don't like pink at all!
I love brown the colour of a tree.
I'm glad I don't like pink.
I like black as well, the colour of a tyre.
I wouldn't like pink!
I like silver ones too, the colour of wheel trims
but
I don't like pink!

Christopher Stone (8)
Woodlands Primary School

THE SEASIDE

I love the seaside.
I love the sand coming between my toes.
I love the sound of the roaring sea.
I love the ice-cream van, when it pulls up on the beach.
I love swimming in the lovely blue sea.
I love playing in the sand.
I love everything about the seaside do you?

Amy Raybould (9)
Woodlands Primary School

MY FAMILY

My sister Jodie talks too much.
She's always making a mess.
She talks too fast and talks too much.
Who would like a sister like that?
She's as skinny as a stick.
My sister Claire she's always hitting me.
She's always playing her music too loud.
My mum she gives me what I want.
She feeds me every day.
She takes me for some fresh air.

Jade Carter (9)
Woodlands Primary School

AMY'S BIRTHDAY

B irthdays are nice
I nside the house .
R ipping open presents
T ying up balloons
H appy children
D ancing all day
A nd they're singing happy birthday Amy.
'Y eah!' shouted Amy.

Katie Wainwright (8)
Woodlands Primary School

FAMILY RELATIVES

When my brother's fighting
He hits me on the head,
And that is when I wish that
He really was dead.

When my sister's playing
With her stupid toys,
The only problem is
She doesn't like boys.

When my dad's eating
Like he's doing all the time,
He always looks like he's
Acting like a mime.

When my mum's angry
Just like mums do,
She makes this horrible sound
Which sounds like a *moo*.

Christopher Jones (8)
Woodlands Primary School

BLUE IS THE COLOUR

Blue is the colour of the sea,
Blue is the colour of the sky,
Blue is the colour of the school's spelling books,
Blue is the colour of our literacy trays,
Blue is the colour of my sharpener,
Blue is the colour of my literacy group door,
Blue is the colour of my rubber.

Ryan Cumming (8)
Woodlands Primary School

THE GREEKS

The Greeks were good at pottery.
The Greeks were good at sculptures.
 The Greeks were good at athletics like javelin and archery.
The Greeks were good builders, they built the Parthenon.
The Greeks loved their gods especially Poseidon.
That's what I know about the Greeks.
Before the Romans reached their peak!

Rory Gallen (9)
Woodlands Primary School